tastes of
MALAYSIA
and
SINGAPORE

JACKI PASSMORE

WELDON
PUBLISHING
SYDNEY · HONG KONG · CHICAGO · LONDON

A Kevin Weldon Production

Published by Weldon Publishing
a division of Kevin Weldon & Associates Pty Limited
372 Eastern Valley Way, Willoughby, NSW 2068, Australia

First published 1991

© Copyright: Kevin Weldon & Associates Pty Limited 1991
© Copyright design: Kevin Weldon & Associates Pty Limited 1991

Printed in Singapore by Kyodo Printing Co (S'pore) Pte Ltd

National Library of Australia Cataloguing-in-Publication data

Passmore, Jacki.
Tastes of Malaysia and Singapore.

Includes index.
ISBN 1 86302 120 5.

1. Cookery, Malaysian. 2. Cookery, Singaporean.
I. Title. (Series : Tastes of Asia).

641.59595

Cover photograph: A selection of sambals (recipes pages 46 and 47).

Frontispiece: Ingredients for steamboat (recipe page 12).

Opposite title page: Spiced fish wrapped in banana leaves (recipe page 15).

CONTENTS

APPETISERS

MALAYSIAN SPRING ROLLS
POPIAH

Popiah are a speciality of Penang but popular throughout Malaysia. They are prepared in two ways, one with a fresh pancake wrapper similar to the Lumpia of the Philippines and the other in spring roll wrappers. The latter is deep fried and is somewhat similar to the Chinese Spring Roll, from which it originated.

Makes about 30 pancakes.

Wrappers:
345 g (11 oz) plain flour
100 g (3½ oz) glutinous rice flour
3 cups water
4 eggs
1½ teaspoons salt

Filling:
185 (6 oz) yam bean *(bangkuang)*, or potato
100 g (3½ oz) bamboo shoots (canned)
8 spring onions
1 small cucumber
2-3 green chillies
3 cloves garlic
155 g (5 oz) pork belly
220 g (7 oz) beanshoots
2 eggs
oil
2 cakes hard beancurd
2½ tablespoons sweet bean paste
155 g (5 oz) raw prawns or shrimps
salt
pepper
1 large lettuce
6 fresh red chillies, pounded
bunch of fresh coriander leaves
2 tablespoons dry fried garlic or onions (see page 125)

Sauce:
1 heaped tablespoon plain flour
3 teaspoons brown sugar
1½ tablespoons dark soya sauce
water

4

Prepare sauce first by sifting flour into a hot dry frying pan. Fry to a light golden colour. Sprinkle on sugar and allow to melt slightly then remove from heat. Cool briefly, then add soya sauce and enough water to form a sauce of medium consistency. Beat for 2 minutes to remove any lumps then cook for 2-3 minutes. Remove from heat and pour into several small bowls.

To make wrappers, sift plain flour into a mixing bowl with glutinous rice flour and salt. Stir in water to form a thick paste, then gradually blend in eggs. Beat for 10 minutes, adding water a little at a time until batter is of thin consistency and very smooth. Stand for 20 minutes before cooking.

Peel yam bean and grate. Put into a small saucepan and cover with boiling water. Simmer until tender, then remove from saucepan, reserving liquid. If potato is used, peel, grate and place in a bowl. Cover with boiling water and stand for 5-6 minutes. Drain, reserving liquid.

Shred bamboo shoots finely. Thinly slice or shred spring onions. Wipe cucumber and grate. Thinly slice chillies and garlic.

Chop pork into 1 cm (½ inch) dice and put into a small saucepan. Cover with water and bring to the boil. Cook on high heat for 10 minutes, then remove, reserving stock. Mince meat.

Soften beanshoots by steeping in boiling water for 2 minutes. Drain and rinse in cold water. Drain again.

Beat eggs lightly. Oil a small omelette pan and pour in eggs. Cook until firm, turn and lightly brown other side. Remove from pan. Cool and shred finely. Shred beancurd.

Heat 2 tablespoons oil in a large frying pan or *wok* and fry sliced garlic for 2 minutes. Add minced pork and brown well. Add yam bean or potato, bamboo shoots and bean paste. Stir well, then pour on ⅓ cup liquid from the cooked yam bean and ⅓ cup liquid from the pork. Simmer on high heat for 10 minutes, until liquid has dried up. Add prawns in last few minutes of cooking. Stir in cucumber, chilli, beancurd and spring onions. Mix well and cook on low heat, stirring frequently, for 3 minutes. Season with salt and pepper. Wash lettuce leaves and wipe dry.

To cook pancake wrappers, brush an omelette pan lightly with oil. Heat and pour in just enough batter to very thinly coat the surface of the pan. Cook on moderate heat until golden underneath with slight specks of brown appearing. Carefully lift up and turn to cook other side. Stack pancakes between pieces of greaseproof paper.

Let pancakes cool slightly, then line each with a lettuce leaf, smear with a little pounded chilli and add several beanshoots. Top with a heaped spoonful of the cooked filling. Garnish with shredded omelette, a few more beanshoots and a sprig of coriander, plus a sprinkling of fried garlic or onion. Roll up tightly, taking care not to tear the pancake. Arrange prepared spring rolls attractively on a wide plate. Serve with the sauce.

If preferred, the lettuce, pancakes, chilli, beanshoots, omelette, herbs and cooked filling may be placed on the table to be individually wrapped.

SPICY YAM RINGS

Makes 18.

500 g (1 lb) yam, taro or sweet potato
2 teaspoons salt
1 teaspoon black pepper
2 heaped teaspoons hot curry powder
½ teaspoon chilli powder
100 g (3½ oz) melted lard (optional)
dry breadcrumbs
oil for shallow frying

Peel yam, taro or sweet potato. Cut into 2.5 cm (1 inch) cubes and place in a steamer to cook until soft. Allow to cool slightly, then mash. Stir in salt, pepper, curry powder and chilli powder and mix to a smooth paste with melted lard. Sweet potato is usually of a much more moist consistency than yam or taro, so if it used, omit lard and substitute a little flour, preferably split pea or gram flour.

Knead for several minutes to distribute the spices evenly, then with oiled hands roll into balls about 4 cm (1½ inches) in diameter. Put on a square of muslin, with space between each. Cover with another piece of cloth and carefully press down to flatten a little. Press the thumb or forefinger through each flattened cake to form a ring. Remove cloth. Smooth edges of each ring and coat thickly with breadcrumbs. Let stand for 15 minutes, in the refrigerator if kitchen is warm.

Heat oil to smoking point, turn heat down very slightly and fry yam rings quickly until crisp on the surface but still soft inside. Lift out and drain on absorbent paper. Serve either warm or cold.

CURRY PUFFS

Makes 24.

500 g (1 lb) prepared puff pastry
100 g (3½ oz) beef or mutton
2 medium potatoes
60 g (2 oz) cooked peas
1 medium onion
2 teaspoons finely chopped fresh coriander leaves
1 cm (½ inch) piece fresh ginger, minced
2 cloves garlic, crushed
2 teaspoons coriander seeds
¼ teaspoon fennel (optional)
1½ teaspoon cummin seeds
2 dried chillies
1 cm (½ inch) stick cinnamon
1 clove
1 teaspoon black peppercorns
1 teaspoon turmeric powder
2 tablespoons *ghee*
1 small onion
2 teaspoons salt
oil for deep frying (optional)

If pastry is frozen, allow to thaw. Chop or mince beef or mutton. Peel potatoes, boil until tender, cool and dice. Drain peas. Chop onion finely. Pound all spices and seasonings into a paste.

Heat *ghee* and fry onion for 3 minutes, add seasoning paste and fry for 4 minutes. Stir in minced meat and cook until well coloured. Stir in potato and peas, heat through, then add chopped tomato and salt. Cover and cook for 4-5 minutes on low heat, stirring frequently to prevent sticking. Remove from heat, and cool completely.

Roll out pastry to 2 mm (1/16 inch) thickness. Divide into 24 circles 10 cm (4 inches) in diameter using a pastry cutter. Place a small amount of filling on one side of each pastry circle. Fold over to form semi-circular pastries. Stick edges down with a little milk or water. Run a pastry wheel around the join, or pinch the wedges into a fluted pattern all around.

Heat oil and deep fry Curry Puffs to a golden brown. Remove from oil, drain and serve either hot or cold. Alternatively, heat oven to 200°C/400°F/Gas Mark 6. Brush pastry tops with a little beaten egg or milk, avoiding sealed edges. Place on a baking sheet and bake for 20-25 minutes. Cool slightly, then remove to a wire rack. Serve hot or cold.

These make excellent hot hors d'oeuvres. Prepare pastry, cutting 5 cm (2 inch) circles, fill and cook as above. Serve on a warming plate or in a chafing dish.

FRIED MALAYSIAN SPRING ROLLS

24 sheets prepared spring roll wrappers (frozen), each
   20 cm (8 inches) square
100 g (3½ oz) raw prawns
100 g (3½ oz) chicken or pork meat
100 g (3½ oz) yam bean *(bangkuang)*, or potato
1 medium carrot
vegetable oil
2 eggs
2 squares hard beancurd
8 spring onions
24 lettuce leaves
4 cloves garlic, crushed
4 green chillies, sliced
pinch monosodium glutamate (optional)
salt
pepper
sugar to taste
3 tablespoons sweet bean paste
1 small cucumber, shredded

Sauce:
2 cloves garlic
2 fresh red chillies
1 teaspoon salt
1½ teaspoons sugar
⅓ cup vinegar
1½ teaspoons water

First prepare sauce. Mince garlic and chillies and mix with remaining ingredients, stirring until sugar dissolves. Add water and pour into several small dishes.

Mince prawns and chicken or pork meat and set aside. Peel and grate yam bean or potato. Put into a saucepan, cover with water and boil till tender. If potato is used, put in a bowl and cover with boiling water. Stand till slightly softened.

Grate carrot, cover with boiling water and cook gently for 2 minutes. Reserve liquid. Lightly oil a small omelette pan. Beat eggs and pour into the pan. Cook until firm, remove and cool, then shred finely.

Add a little more oil to the pan and fry beancurd for 2-3 minutes, turning once, then remove from pan. Cool slightly, then shred. Shred spring onions. Wash lettuce leaves and wipe dry.

Heat 3 tablespoons oil in a large pan and add minced pork or chicken and prawns. Add garlic and fry until meat changes colour. Season with chillies, spring onions, monosodium glutamate (if used), salt and pepper. Cook for 2-3 minutes, stirring occasionally. Add strained vegetables, sugar and bean paste. Cook for 4 minutes, then mix in shredded cucumber and beancurd. Stir continually on high heat for 3 minutes. Pour in a little of the stock in which carrots were cooked, adding just enough to moisten filling. Remove from heat and cool.

Spread a lettuce leaf on each spring roll wrapper. Top with a generous spoonful of filling and garnish with shredded omelette. Roll up carefully and stick edges down by wetting well, or prepare a paste of cornflour and boiling water and use this to stick down the flaps.

Heat 5 cm (2 inches) oil to smoking point, lower heat slightly and put in spring rolls, several at a time. Fry to a deep golden brown. Remove from oil, drain on absorbent paper. Serve with the sauce.

FRIED SEASONED WHITEBAIT
IKAN BILIS

250 g (½ lb) whitebait (dried salted whitebait if
 available)
1 medium onion
2-3 green chillies
1 tablespoon sugar
2 teaspoons ground black peppercorns
salt (optional)
75 g (2½ oz) peanuts
oil for deep frying

If dried salted whitebait *(ikan bilis)* is used, remove
heads and backbones and wash in cold water. Drain
well and shake in a cloth to dry. Fresh whitebait should
be washed and dried, preferably in the sun, for about 1
hour.
 Grind onion, chillies, sugar and peppercorns to a
smooth paste. Set aside. Heat oil and fry whitebait
until very dry and crisp, then transfer to a rack or plate
covered with absorbent paper.
 Pour off oil and add chilli paste to the pan. Fry on
high heat until seasonings begin to dry, then return
whitebait to the pan and cook for a further 6 minutes,
stirring continually. Add salt if fresh fish is used.
 Roast peanuts under griller until crisp and golden
brown. Rub off skins if preferred. Add to the pan and
stir on high heat for another minute. Mix with fried
whitebait. Spoon into small dishes and serve as a crisp,
tasty side dish with meat or vegetable curries, or as a
snack with drinks.

SOUPS

CHICKEN AND NOODLE SOUP

LAKSA AYAM

1½ tablespoons peanut oil
6 candlenuts, ground
2 teaspoons chilli powder
1 heaped teaspoon cummin, ground
4 cloves garlic, minced
1 large onion, minced
1 large tomato, chopped
1 teaspoon sugar
2½ teaspoons salt
½ teaspoon white pepper
9 cups thin coconut milk
500 g (1 lb) thin rice vermicelli
250 g (½ lb) beanshoots
250 g (½ lb) cooked chicken meat, shredded
60 g (2 oz) fried hard beancurd, shredded
6 spring onions, chopped
¾ cup thick coconut milk
2 green chillies, thinly sliced
fresh coriander leaves, chopped

Heat oil in a *wok* or frying pan and fry ground candle-nuts with chilli powder, cummin, garlic and onion for 4 minutes, stirring constantly. Add chopped tomato, sugar, salt and pepper, then pour on thin coconut milk and bring almost to the boil. Turn heat down low and simmer for 6-8 minutes, then set aside, keeping warm.

Pour boiling water over rice vermicelli and leave for about 8 minutes until softened. Drain and rinse with cold water. Drain again. Steep beanshoots in boiling water for 2 minutes. Drain and rinse. To serve, divide rice noodles between six large bowls. Top each with a serving of beanshoots, shredded chicken, fried bean-curd and spring onion. Pour on a little thick coconut milk and a generous amount of the coconut sauce.

Garnish with sliced chilli and chopped coriander. Soya sauce or extra salt may be added, to taste.

MUTTON SOUP
SOP KAMBING

750 g (1½ lb) mutton ribs
2 large onions, chopped
3 cloves garlic, crushed
2 green chillies, sliced
1 heaped teaspoon grated *lengkuas* or fresh ginger
2 teaspoons black peppercorns
3 teaspoons coriander seeds
9 cups water
1 tablespoon oil
4 black cardamoms, lightly crushed
5 cm (2 inch) stick cinnamon
2-3 cloves
2.5 cm (1 inch) piece fresh ginger, grated
3 tablespoons mild curry powder or paste
2 heaped tablespoons white poppy seeds
½ cup thick coconut milk
salt
pepper
dry fried onions
spring onion, chopped
fresh coriander leaves

Chop mutton bones into 5 cm (2 inch) pieces. Put in a large saucepan with onion, garlic, chilli, *lengkuas* or ginger, peppercorns and coriander. Cover with water and bring to the boil. Turn heat down, cover and simmer for 2½-3 hours. Skim off froth as it rises.

Strain stock, reserving liquid (which should be reduced to about 5 cups) and meat. When cool, scrape meat from bones and flake into smaller pieces.

Heat oil in a saucepan and fry cardamoms, cinnamon, cloves and ginger for 1 minute, then add curry powder or paste and fry for 4 minutes. Pour in lightly ground poppy seeds, coconut milk and add reserved stock. Stir well. Season with salt and pepper to taste. Add meat, bring to the boil and cook for 20 minutes.

Serve soup in a tureen or in individual bowls garnished with dry fried onions, spring onion and coriander leaves.

STEAMBOAT

A popular meal in Singapore. Steamboat derives its name from the charcoal-heated pot with funnel chimney in which food is cooked at the table.

10 cups chicken stock
½ teaspoon monosodium glutamate (optional)
2 tablespoons vegetable oil
2.5 cm (1 inch) piece fresh ginger, sliced
1 fresh red or green chilli, sliced
8 spring onions, chopped
12 medium raw prawns
125 g (¼ lb) pork, leg or shoulder
125 g (¼ lb) rump, sirloin or fillet steak
125 g (¼ lb) chicken breast
250 g (½ lb) fish fillets (bream, perch, whiting)
125 g (¼ lb) cuttlefish (optional)
large bunch fresh spinach, lettuce or Chinese cabbage
    leaves
6 eggs (optional)
chilli sauce
3 tablespoons light soya sauce
3 cloves garlic
2.5 cm (1 inch) piece fresh ginger, shredded
2 teaspoons sugar

Bring stock to a rapid boil and add monosodium glutamate (if used), vegetable oil, ginger, sliced chilli and onions. Turn heat down and simmer for 10 minutes, then pour into the Steamboat or other suitable pot which can be heated at the table.

Peel and devein prawns, leaving tails on. Slice pork, beef and chicken thinly. Cut fish fillets into thin strips. Clean and slice cuttlefish. Wash vegetables and shake out excess water. Separate leaves. Arrange meat, prawns and fish attractively on a plate with the vegetables. Keep eggs aside.

Mix soya sauce, crushed garlic, shredded ginger and sugar, stirring till sugar is dissolved. Pour into several small dishes. Spoon chilli sauce into several small dishes.

When stock begins to bubble, the ingredients are cooked individually at the table by each diner, using wooden chopsticks or small wire baskets. Fondue forks could be used. Dip cooked food into either of the sauces.

When all ingredients have been consumed, carefully break the eggs into the stock and poach lightly. These are eaten with the remaining highly enriched soup.

Opposite: Singapore chilli crab (recipe page 19).
Overleaf: Tamarind prawns, and curried cuttlefish (recipes pages 18 and 20).

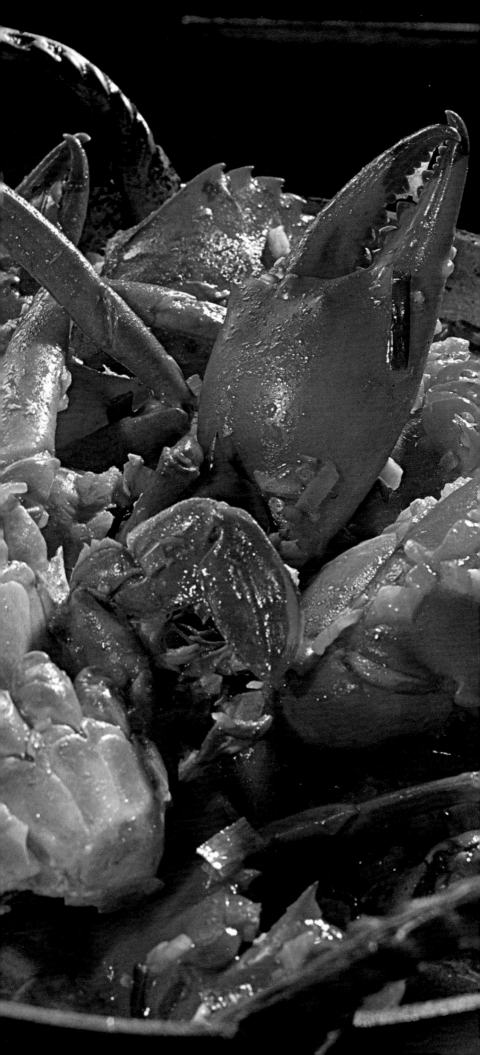

CHINESE SOUP WITH PICKLED VEGETABLES, BEANCURD AND MIXED MEAT

I discovered this delicious soup at an outdoor restaurant on the waterfront in Malacca city.

2 squares soft beancurd
185 g (6 oz) mixed, pickled vegetables (canned)
2 medium tomatoes
1 medium cucumber
6 raw prawns (optional)
2 teaspoons Chinese wine
100 g (3½ oz) chicken, diced
100 g (3½ oz) pork, shredded
8 cups cold water
salt
pepper
pinch monosodium glutamate (optional)
6 spring onions, shredded
small bunch fresh coriander leaves
2 green chillies (optional)

Drain beancurd and cut into thin slices. Drain pickled vegetables and rinse in cold water to remove excess salt. Slice or chop roughly. Wipe tomato and cucumber and cut into even sized pieces. Peel and devein prawns, sprinkle with Chinese wine and marinate for 10 minutes.

Put diced chicken and shredded pork in a large pot with pickled vegetables. Cover with cold water and bring to the boil. Lower heat slightly and simmer for 10 minutes. Add cucumber, tomatoes and prawns and cook for 6 minutes. Season to taste with salt and pepper and add monosodium glutamate (if used).

Just before serving, add sliced beancurd and spring onions. Heat through. Garnish with coriander leaves and shredded chilli.

13

SEAFOOD

DRY FRIED FISH

This crispy fish is served as a side dish with curries and other dishes of Malay origin and is accompanied by a chilli and vinegar or onion sambal.

750 g (1½ lb) very small red mullet, herrings or whiting
2 teaspoons salt
2 teaspoons chilli powder
2 tablespoons cornflour
peanut or vegetable oil for deep frying
soya sauce (optional)

Clean fish, leaving heads on. Wash and wipe dry and season inside and out with a mixture of salt and chilli powder. Coat lightly with cornflour, shaking off excess.
  Heat oil in a *wok* or large pan and when very hot put in several small fish. Fry to a deep golden brown, turning heat down slightly after first minute.
  Remove from oil when cooked and crisp and drain well. Cook remaining fish and set all aside to cool.
  Just before serving heat a dry frying pan or *wok* and cook fish for 1 minute on each side, adding a splash of soya sauce if desired.

SOUR FISH

IKAN ASAM

375 g (¾ lb) fish fillets
1½ tablespoons tamarind
3 cups boiling water
4 candlenuts
1 stalk lemon grass
1 teaspoon grated fresh turmeric or
    ½ teaspoon turmeric powder
½ teaspoon dried shrimp paste
6 spring onions, chopped
6 fresh red chillies, finely chopped
2 tablespoons peanut or vegetable oil
salt

Cut fish into strips about 2 cm by 5 cm (¾ inch by 2 inches). Soak tamarind in boiling water. Pound ginger and candlenuts in a mortar or spice grinder together with lemon grass, turmeric, dried shrimp paste, spring onions and chopped chillies.
Add strained tamarind water with lemon grass, chilli, turmeric and salt. Bring to the boil, turn heat down and stir in thin coconut milk. When the sauce is almost boiling drop in fish slices and pour on thick coconut milk. Simmer for about 5 minutes until fish is tender.
  Check seasonings, adding more salt if necessary. Spoon into a serving dish and garnish with chopped coriander leaves.

14

SPICED FISH WRAPPED IN BANANA LEAVES
OTAK OTAK

500 g (1 lb) white fish fillets
4 candlenuts
2 medium onions, minced
2 cloves garlic, minced
¼ teaspoon turmeric powder or 1 teaspoon grated fresh
  turmeric
2.5 cm (1 inch) piece fresh ginger, minced
½ teaspoon tamarind
1 teaspoon salt
1 tablespoon chilli powder
2 teaspoons coriander, ground
2 teaspoons cummin, ground
½ teaspoon *daun kesom*, chopped
banana leaves (or aluminium foil)

Cut fish into thin slices about 1 cm (½ inch) thick and
10 cm by 5 cm (4 inches by 2 inches). Grind candlenuts
and mix to a paste with all the remaining ingredients,
except banana leaves. Hold banana leaves over a flame
to soften.
   Coat each fish slice thickly with the ground ingredients and wrap in a small piece of well-greased banana
leaf. Secure with toothpicks. Grill or toast over a charcoal fire for 8-10 minutes.
   Serve with the leaf partially torn away to display the
fish.

FISH MOOLEE

750 g (1½ lb) cod, haddock or snapper
1 tablespoon tamarind
1¼ cups boiling water
2 cloves garlic
5 shallots
2 tablespoons oil
2.5 cm (1 inch) piece fresh ginger
1 stalk lemon grass
1 fresh red chilli, thinly sliced
½ teaspoon turmeric powder
1 teaspoon salt
¾ cup thin coconut milk
¾ cup thick coconut milk
fresh coriander leaves, chopped

Cut fish into fillets and remove skin. Cut fillets into
pieces about 5 cm (2 inches) square. Soak tamarind in
boiling water. Chop garlic and shallots finely. Shred
ginger.
   Heat oil in a pan and fry garlic and shallots for 2
minutes. Add ginger and cook for another minute.
   Heat oil and fry pounded mixture for 4 minutes.
Pour in strained tamarind water and bring to the boil.
Turn heat down and simmer for 8 minutes. Add fish
slices and cook on low heat for about 3 minutes until
tender.
   Transfer fish to a serving plate. Season sauce with salt
and strain through a fine sieve over the fish.
   Large unpeeled prawns may also be cooked in this
way. Serve the fish without the sauce if it is to accompany other dishes with sauce.

STEAMED FISH WITH CHILLI SAUCE

750 g (1½ lb) pomfret, bream or snapper
salt
1 tablespoon oil
1 large onion, finely chopped
2 cloves garlic, crushed
2 teaspoons minced ginger
1 tomato
2-3 fresh red chillies, finely chopped
1 teaspoon chilli powder
1 tablespoon white vinegar
1 tablespoon sugar
½ cup cold water
1 heaped teaspoon cornflour
fresh coriander or parsley sprigs

Clean and scale fish and make several deep diagonal incisions across each side. Rub with salt. Put on a flat, lightly oiled plate and steam over boiling water for 8 minutes, or until cooked through. Test by inserting a toothpick into the thickest part. If no pinkish liquid escapes the fish is done.

Heat oil and cook onion with garlic until soft but not coloured. Add ginger and cook for another minute. Chop tomato and add to the pan with chopped chillies, chilli powder, vinegar, sugar and water. Bring to the boil, turn heat down and simmer for 4 minutes. Season with salt. Mix cornflour with a little cold water and stir into the sauce. Cook until sauce thickens and clears.

Place steamed fish on an oval serving plate and pour on the hot sauce. Garnish with sprigs of coriander or parsley.

PRAWN AND CABBAGE CURRY

375 g (¾ lb) Chinese cabbage, or white cabbage
6 shallots, finely chopped
1 clove garlic, finely chopped
2 tablespoons oil
250 g (½ lb) peeled raw prawns
1 teaspoon turmeric powder
2 teaspoons salt
¾ cup thin coconut milk
¾ cup thick coconut milk

Chop cabbage roughly, discarding centre stalk. Rinse in cold water and shake dry. Heat oil in a large saucepan or *wok* and fry shallots and garlic until soft but not coloured. Add cabbage and prawns to the pan and saute for 3 minutes, stirring frequently.

Stir in turmeric and salt, then pour on thin coconut milk and bring almost to the boil. Add thick coconut milk, turn down heat and simmer for about 4 minutes. Cabbage should still be slightly crisp.

This is a very mild curry. Sprinkle on 1-2 teaspoons chilli powder for a slightly hotter taste. Halved hard-boiled eggs may be added when curry is almost done.

MALACCAN FISH CURRY, PORTUGESE STYLE

500 g (1 lb) fillets of cod, haddock or snapper
2 medium onions
6 cloves garlic
5 cm (2 inch) piece fresh ginger
250 g (½ lb) tomatoes
3 green chillies
3 tablespoons vegetable or peanut oil
½ teaspoon cummin
2 teaspoons fennel
½ cup water
1 tablespoon tamarind
1 stalk lemon grass
5 curry leaves
2-3 tablespoons curry powder
1 teaspoon chilli powder
½ teaspoon turmeric powder, or
   1½ teaspoons grated fresh turmeric
1½ cups warm water or fish stock
salt
cornflour
dry fried onions

Cut each fish fillet into 2-3 pieces. Peel onions and garlic and chop finely. Shred ginger. Slice tomatoes and chillies.

Heat oil in a large saucepan and fry cummin, fennel, ginger, onion and garlic for 3 minutes. Add tomato and half the chillies and fry for a further 2 minutes. Soak tamarind in water, squeeze, strain and add together with chopped lemon grass and curry leaves. Cook for 2 minutes. Sprinkle on curry powder, chilli powder, turmeric and pour on warm water or fish stock. Stir thoroughly and bring to the boil.

Coat fish fillets lightly with salt and cornflour and drop into the boiling sauce. Cook on moderate heat for 6 minutes, then remove fish and set aside.

Bring sauce to the boil and simmer until it reduces and thickens slightly. Thicken with a little cornflour if necessary. Add salt to taste. Return fish to the sauce, reheat and then spoon onto a serving dish.

Garnish with the remaining sliced green chillies and a little dry fried onion.

TAMARIND PRAWNS
UDANG ASAM

2 tablespoons tamarind
1 cup boiling water
500 g (1 lb) large raw prawns
2 teaspoons chilli powder
2 teaspoons sugar
2 tablespoons oil
185 g (6 oz) mixed pickled vegetables, or
    sliced tomato and cucumber

Soak tamarind in boiling water for 30 minutes. Remove shell from prawns, leaving heads and tails intact. Carefully scrape out dark veins with a sharp knife, then make deep incisions down the centre back of the prawns to make them curl up during cooking. Arrange prawns in a wide flat bowl. Strain tamarind water, and stir in chilli powder and sugar. Pour over prawns and marinate for up to 1 hour, turning occasionally.

Heat oil in a *wok* or large frying pan. Drain prawns and saute on high heat for 2 minutes. Pour on marinade and cook until prawns are tender. Remove prawns from sauce with a slotted spoon. Bring sauce to the boil and cook until well reduced.

Drain pickled vegetables and arrange these, or tomato and cucumber slices, around the edge of a serving dish. Place prawns in the centre and pour on the sauce.

PRAWNS IN GINGER

500 g (1 lb) large raw prawns
2 teaspoons salt
5 cm (2 inch) piece fresh ginger, finely shredded
1 teaspoon finely ground black pepper
2 tablespoons Chinese win
1 teaspoon sesame oil
vegetable oil for deep frying
pineapple chunks

Clean, peel, and devein prawns, and remove heads. Wash and dry well. Season with salt and roll in shredded ginger, coating well. Allow to stand for 7 minutes to absorb the ginger flavour.

Heat oil in a deep pan and lower prawns in on a slotted spoon. Deep fry until cooked through, then remove and drain. Do not overcook or prawns will become tough and dry.

Pour out all but 1 tablespoon oil and add remaining ingredients to the pan, including any leftover ginger. Boil for 30 seconds, then return prawns and saute for another 30 seconds.

Arrange prawns on a serving plate and garnish with pineapple chunks.

SINGAPORE CHILLI CRAB

2 medium raw crabs
3 teaspoons tamarind
¾ cup boiling water
3 tablespoons oil
2 medium onions, minced
5 cm (2 inch) piece fresh ginger, minced
4 fresh red chillies, finely chopped
1-2 teaspoons chilli powder
2 teaspoons tomato paste
3 teaspoons sugar, or to taste
2 teaspoons cornflour
fresh red and green chillies, sliced
spring onions, chopped

Drop crabs into boiling, slightly salted water and cook rapidly for 4 minutes. Remove, drain and leave to cool. Soak tamarind in boiling water. Chop crabs into large pieces, if possible leaving the legs attached to the body pieces. Remove the spongey grey portion and discard.
   Heat oil in a *wok* or very large pan and saute onion, ginger and chopped chillies for 2 minutes. Add crab pieces and sprinkle on chilli powder, then pour in strained tamarind water. Lower heat and simmer for 4 minutes.
   Remove crab to a serving plate. Add tomato paste and sugar to the sauce. Thicken with cornflour mixed with a little cold water and cook until sauce thickens and clears slightly. Pour over crab.
   Garnish with sliced chilli and spring onion.

CRAB CURRY

KETAM MASAK LEMAK

6 small raw crabs
3-4 green chillies
1 teaspoon turmeric powder
10 cm (4 inch) piece lemon grass, finely sliced
4 cm (1½ inch) piece fresh ginger, shredded
1½ teaspoons salt
1¾ cups thick coconut milk

Wash crabs, wipe dry and crack open shells underneath. Remove all inedible parts and rinse again. Using a heavy knife handle or the flat blade of a cleaver crack shells and claws to allow the seasonings to penetrate the meat.
   Chop chillies finely. Arrange crabs in a large saucepan and sprinkle on chopped chilli, turmeric, lemon grass, ginger and salt. Pour on coconut milk. Set on moderate heat and simmer, covered, until crabs are cooked and sauce thick and well flavoured.

CRABMEAT OMELETTE
FOO YUNG HAI

4 shallots or 6 spring onions
½ small carrot
30 g (1 oz) bamboo shoot
4 large eggs
1 tablespoon sago or potato flour
2 tablespoons oil
60 g (2 oz) Chinese cabbage, roughly chopped
185 g (6 oz) fresh crabmeat, shredded
2 teaspoons chilli powder (optional)
salt
pepper
monosodium glutamate (optional)
6 sprigs coriander
1 spring onion, shredded

Finely chop shallots or spring onions. Grate or finely chop carrot and bamboo shoot. Beat eggs lightly with sago or potato flour and set aside.

Heat oil in a large frying pan. Fry shallots or spring onions for 2 minutes, then add carrot, bamboo shoots and cabbage. Cook for 3 minutes. Scatter on crabmeat and season with chilli powder (if used), salt and pepper and a pinch of monosodium glutamate (if used). Fry for 1 minute, then pour in eggs and lower heat. Stir gently to mix eggs evenly with vegetables and crabmeat, then cover and cook until just set.

Lift onto a serving plate and garnish with coriander and shredded spring onion. Serve with chilli oil or chilli sauce.

CURRIED CUTTLEFISH

500 g (1 lb) small fresh cuttlefish or squid
1 heaped teaspoon tamarind
¾ cup boiling water
1 small onion, minced
2 cloves garlic, crushed
1 cm (½ inch) piece fresh ginger, minced
1 tablespoon curry powder
2 tablespoons oil
1 tablespoon tomato paste
2 teaspoons sugar
salt
pepper
½ cup thick coconut milk

Clean cuttlefish and remove skin and intestines. Discard heads and ink bags. Soak tamarind in boiling water, then strain and pour liquid over cuttlefish. Marinate for 10 minutes.

Mix together onion, garlic, ginger and curry powder and fry in oil for 5 minutes, stirring frequently. Put in cuttlefish and tamarind water, stir well, then add tomato paste, sugar and salt and pepper to taste. Bring to the boil and simmer for 2 minutes. Pour in coconut milk, turn heat down low and simmer for a further 1½ minutes.

CHICKEN

MALAY CHICKEN

1 kg (2 lb) chicken
12 dried chillies, soaked
1 tablespoon curry paste or powder
1 teaspoon turmeric powder
1 teaspoon cummin
1-2 cloves garlic, chopped
5 shallots or 2 medium red onions, chopped
2 tablespoons oil
1 teaspoon sugar
1½ cups thick coconut milk
2 large tomatoes, sliced
1 red onion, thinly sliced
2-3 spring onions, shredded, or
    6 sprigs coriander leaf
sliced tomato
sliced cucumber
dry fried onion

Clean chicken, wipe dry and chop into medium sized pieces. Pound soaked chillies, curry paste or powder, turmeric, cummin, garlic and shallots or onion to a fairly smooth paste.

Heat oil in a heavy saucepan and fry seasonings for 3 minutes. Put in chicken and fry for 8 minutes, stirring to colour evenly. Sprinkle on sugar and pour in coconut milk.

Simmer on a moderate heat until chicken is tender and coconut milk well reduced. Add tomato and onion slices and shredded spring onion or coriander and cook for 5 minutes, stirring frequently.

Spoon onto a serving dish and surround with slices of tomato and cucumber. Sprinkle on fried onion (if used).

FRIED SPICED CHICKEN

1.25 kg (2½ lb) chicken
salt
1 heaped teaspoon cummin, ground
2 heaped teaspoons coriander, ground
1 heaped teaspoon turmeric powder
2-3 teaspoons chilli powder
3 teaspoons sugar
5 cm (2 inch) piece fresh ginger, shredded
2 tablespoons lemon juice or tamarind water
oil for deep frying
lettuce leaves
krupuk or potato crisps

Clean chicken, chop into fairly large pieces and wipe dry. Sprinkle generously with salt. Mix all remaining seasonings into a paste and rub well into the chicken pieces. Allow to stand for 45 minutes to absorb the flavours.

Heat oil in a deep pan and when almost at smoking point carefully lower the chicken pieces into the oil. Turn heat down slightly. Fry chicken until cooked through and well crisped on the surface. Remove from oil and drain thoroughly on absorbent paper.

Serve on a bed of lettuce and garnish with freshly fried *krupuk* or potato crisps.

21

SWEET CHICKEN CURRY

BEGUM BEHAR

1.25 kg (2½ lb) chicken
3 tablespoons *ghee* or butter
1 large onion, minced
2 cloves garlic, minced
1 cm (½ inch) piece fresh ginger, minced
1 teaspoon turmeric powder
2½ teaspoons coriander, ground
3 cloves
1 teaspoon chilli powder
1½ teaspoons sugar
1 teaspoon crushed peppercorns
1½ teaspoons cummin, ground
1 bay leaf
1 cup water
1 tomato, chopped
30 g (1 oz) sultanas, soaked in water
3 tablespoons thick cream
2 hardboiled eggs, chopped
30 g (1 oz) roasted, slivered almonds

Clean chicken and chop into medium sized pieces. Heat *ghee* or butter and gently fry onion, garlic and ginger for 3 minutes, then add turmeric, coriander, slightly crushed cloves, chilli powder, sugar, peppercorns, cummin and bay leaf. Saute for 2 minutes, then put in chicken pieces. Turn heat up slightly and cook, stirring frequently, until chicken takes on a good colour.

Pour in ½ cup water, turn heat down and simmer for 10 minutes. Add tomato and drained sultanas and another ½ cup water. Cover and cook until chicken is very tender. Stir in cream and chopped boiled eggs. Heat through, then spoon onto a serving dish. Garnish with slivered almonds.

CAPTAIN'S CURRY

KARI KAPITAN

1.25 kg (2½ lb) chicken
2 teaspoons dried shrimp paste
10 cm (4 inch) stalk lemon grass, chopped
6 candlenuts
1 tablespoon coriander, ground
2.5 cm (1 inch) piece fresh ginger, shredded
1½ teaspoons grated fresh turmeric or
   ¾ teaspoon turmeric powder
3 small red onions, or 6 shallots
3 cloves garlic
2 tablespoons oil
1½ cups thin coconut milk
3 teaspoons sugar
salt
pepper
4 spring onions, shredded

Clean chicken, rinse with cold water and wipe dry.
Chop into pieces about 5 cm (2 inches) square, or, if
preferred cut all meat from bones.

Make a paste with dried shrimp paste, lemon grass,
candlenuts, coriander, cinnamon, ginger and turmeric,
grinding ingredients in a mortar or on a grinding stone.
Alternatively, grind dry spices in a coffee grinder and
add shredded ginger. Chop onions or shallots and garlic
finely.

Heat oil in a *wok* or deep saucepan and fry onion and
garlic until soft. Add seasoning paste and fry for 3
minutes, stirring frequently. Remove from the heat and
stir in coconut milk. Add chicken pieces to coconut
milk and seasonings. Sprinkle on sugar and season with
salt and pepper. Cover and cook gently until chicken is
very tender, literally falling off the bones, and sauce
thick.

Garnish with shredded spring onion.

HAINANESE STYLE CHICKEN

1.25 kg (2 ½ lb) chicken
4 spring onions, minced
2.5 cm (1 inch) piece fresh ginger, minced
2 teaspoons Chinese rice wine
3 teaspoons salt
3 tablespoons vegetable oil
375 g (¾ lb) rice
8 cups light chicken stock
250 g (½ lb) Chinese vegetables (cabbage or spring
   greens)
salt
soya sauce

Sauce:
2 tablespoons vegetable oil
2 spring onions, finely shredded
5 cm (2 inch) piece fresh ginger, finely shredded

Clean chicken and wipe dry. Mix onions and ginger
with wine and salt. Rub outside and cavity of chicken
with the seasonings and allow to stand for 1 hour. Place
chicken in a covered dish over a steamer and steam on a
high heat for 35-40 minutes. Allow to cool slightly,
then remove and chop into bite-sized pieces. Arrange
on a plate and set aside.

Wash rice well then drain thoroughly. Heat 3 tablespoons oil and fry rice for 5 minutes, stirring to coat
each grain with oil. Pour in cold water to cover rice by 4
cm (1 ½ inches). Cover the pan, bring to the boil, then
turn heat down to lowest point and cook until rice is
tender and liquid completely absorbed.

Bring chicken stock to the boil, add washed vegetables and simmer for 1 minute. Lift out and drain.
Season soup to taste with salt and soya sauce. Mix together sauce ingredients and spoon into tiny dishes.

Serve the chicken warm or cold with rice, the hot
stock as a soup, the vegetables and the sauce.

Mutton and eggplant curry (recipe page 27).

FRIED PENANG CHICKEN
INCHE KABIN

1 kg (2 lb) chicken
2.5 cm (1 inch) piece fresh ginger, sliced
2 teaspoons chilli paste (see below)
2 teaspoons turmeric powder
1 tablespoon lemon or lime juice
1 teaspoon sugar
½ cup thick coconut milk
peanut oil for deep frying
12 large freshly fried *krupuk*

Chilli Paste:
1 fresh red chilli
½ teaspoon salt
½ teaspoon sugar
½ tablespoon oil

Finely chop or mince chilli and mix with remaining ingredients.

Sauce:
¼ cup Lea and Perrins or Worcestershire sauce
2 teaspoons hot mustard powder
sugar to taste
lemon or lime juice

Clean chicken, wipe dry and cut into 6 pieces. Prepare ginger juice by infusing sliced ginger in 1 tablespoon boiling water. Prepare chilli paste and mix with ginger juice, turmeric, lemon or lime juice and sugar. Rub the seasonings into the chicken pieces and stand ½ hour, turning occasionally. Remove from marinade and drain well.

Heat oil and when almost at smoking point fry chicken on very high heat until deep brown in colour. Remove chicken from oil and allow to cool. Turn off heat, but keep the oil in the pan.

When chicken is cool, heat oil until moderately hot and return chicken to the pan. Cook for 8-10 minutes, or until meat is cooked through. Test with a skewer in the thickest parts of the chicken. If no pink liquid runs off the chicken is done. Do not overcook.

Remove chicken from oil and allow to stand for 5 minutes, then return to the marinade. Soak for 10 minutes in this liquid, then drain.

Turn heat up very high and when oil is very hot drop in chicken pieces and cook quickly till the surface of the chicken is very dark brown. Remove from oil, drain and arrange on a serving plate. Surround with freshly fried *krupuk*.

Mix sauce ingredients together in a small bowl, stirring to thoroughly dissolve sugar and mustard. Add a little water and lime or lemon juice to taste.

Sweet chicken curry, and coconut rice (recipes pages 22 and 39).

LAMB AND MUTTON

LAMB CURRY

KARI KAMBING

625 g (1¼ lb) lamb, shoulder or leg
2 cloves garlic
2 teaspoons peanut oil or *ghee*
4 shallots or 2 small red onions, finely chopped
2½ tablespoons mild curry powder
2 teaspoons salt
1 teaspoon crushed black peppercorns
1½ cups warm water
2 medium potatoes, parboiled
1¾ cups thin coconut milk
½ cup thick coconut milk
90 g (3 oz) cooked peas (optional)
3 hardboiled eggs
fresh coriander leaves, mint or parsley, chopped

Chop meat into 2 cm (¾ inch) cubes. Crush garlic.
Heat oil in a deep pan and saute shallots or onion and
garlic until soft but not coloured. Add curry powder
with salt and peppercorns and fry for 2 minutes. Pour in
½ cup water and stir well. Add cubed lamb and cook
for 5 minutes, stirring frequently. Pour in remaining
water and simmer on moderate heat, stirring occasionally, until all liquid has evaporated and meat is tender.

Cut potatoes into 2.5 cm (1 inch) cubes and add to
the pan with thin coconut milk. Simmer for 5 minutes,
then pour in thick coconut milk and add peas and
halved boiled eggs. Heat through, remove from heat
and let stand for 2 hours. Reheat before serving. Spoon
into a serving bowl and sprinkle with chopped herbs.

MUTTON AND EGGPLANT CURRY

500 g (1 lb) lean mutton or lamb, shoulder or leg
3 medium eggplants
salt
1½ tablespoons white poppy seeds
1 teaspoon fennel seeds, crushed
3 teaspoons coriander, ground
1¼ teaspoons cummin, ground
1½ teaspoons black peppercorns, crushed
¾ teaspoon turmeric powder or
   1½ teaspoons grated fresh turmeric
2.5 cm (1 inch) piece fresh ginger
8 shallots or 3 small red onions
3 cloves garlic
4 tablespoons *ghee* or oil
3 curry leaves, or 1 bay leaf
3 cloves
2 cm (¾ inch) stick cinnamon
2 cups thin coconut milk
½ cup thick coconut milk
lime juice or wedges of fresh lime

Chop meat into 2 cm (¾ inch) cubes. Remove stems from eggplants, wipe with a clean cloth and cut in halves lengthways, then into 5 cm (2 inch) pieces. Sprinkle with salt, cover and allow to stand for 10 minutes to draw bitter juices.

Grind poppy seeds, fennel, coriander, cummin and peppercorns together and mix with turmeric. Peel ginger and shred finely. Mince shallots or onions and garlic. Heat *ghee* or oil in a large pan and fry onions and garlic with ginger for 3 minutes. Add ground seasonings and fry for 5 minutes, stirring frequently. Put in cubed meat, curry or bay leaves, cloves and cinnamon stick. Cook on moderate heat for 10 minutes, stirring to coat meat with seasonings.

Rinse eggplants, wipe and add to the pan, cooking for another 5 minutes. Pour on thin coconut milk and bring almost to the boil. Lower heat and cook for about 25 minutes until meat and eggplant are tender. Stir in thick coconut milk and cook until sauce thickens slightly.

Season to taste with salt and lime juice. Spoon into a serving dish. If serving with lime wedges, arrange around the edge of the dish.

Note: If using mutton, do not add eggplant when frying meat. Simmer meat in thin coconut milk until almost tender, then add eggplant and cook for another 20-25 minutes before adding thick coconut milk.

BEEF

TAMARIND BEEF

DAGING ASAM

625 g (1¼ lb) chuck, round or topside steak
6 dried chillies, soaked
10 shallots, chopped
2.5 cm (1 inch) piece fresh ginger
4 candlenuts
1 teaspoon dried shrimp paste
½ teaspoon turmeric powder
2 tablespoons oil
3 cups water
2 tablespoons tamarind
sugar
salt
1 fresh red chilli, finely sliced
1 green chilli, finely sliced

Cut beef into small pieces. Chop or mince dried chillies, shallots and ginger and grind to a paste with candlenuts, dried shrimp paste and turmeric.

Heat oil in a large pan and fry seasonings for 4 minutes, stirring constantly. Put in beef and turn several times to thoroughly coat meat pieces with the seasonings. Fry until well browned. Soak tamarind in water. Squeeze and strain into meat. Bring to the boil, then add sugar and salt to taste. Turn heat down and simmer till beef is very tender and gravy slightly reduced.

Remove beef and arrange on a serving dish. Pour on a little of the sauce. Garnish with sliced red and green chillies. Serve the meat without sauce if it is to accompany other sauced dishes.

CHINESE BEEF WITH SPRING ONIONS

250 g (½ lb) rump, sirloin or topside steak
1 tablespoon Chinese rice wine
pinch of monosodium glutamate (optional)
1 tablespoon cornflour
2 cloves garlic
12 spring onions
2 tablespoons oil
4 cm (1½ inch) piece fresh ginger, finely shredded
3 teaspoons sugar
2 tablespoons dark soya sauce
2-3 tablespoons beef stock
1 green chilli, thinly sliced

Slice meat very thinly, then cut into pieces about 5 cm by 2 cm (2 inches by ¾ inch). Sprinkle on Chinese wine and monosodium glutamate (if used) and stand for 10 minutes. Coat lightly with cornflour, shaking off excess.

Chop garlic finely. Clean spring onions, discarding green ends and cut into 5 cm (2 inch) pieces. Heat oil in a *wok* and when very hot put in meat, garlic and ginger. Stir-fry for 2 minutes, then sprinkle on sugar, soya sauce and stock. Add spring onions. Cook until meat is tender and most of the liquid has been absorbed.

Spoon onto a serving dish and garnish with sliced green chilli. This meat dish makes an ideal topping for fried noodles.

DRIED BEEF

DENDENG

375 g (¾ lb) sirloin, round or rump steak
1 large onion
1 stalk lemon grass
4 cm (1½ inch) piece *lengkuas*
2 teaspoons sugar
1 teaspoon salt
oil for deep frying
2 fresh red chillies
1-2 green chillies
4 shallots

Cut beef into paper thin slices with a very sharp knife, cutting across the grain. Peel onion and mince. Chop lemon grass, then pound to a coarse paste with *lengkuas*. Mix in onion, sugar and salt. Coat meat with the seasoning paste and arrange on a wide bamboo or wooden rack. Lay out in hot sunlight for about 30-40 minutes. Alternatively place in a moderate oven for 20 minutes, turning once.

Heat oil and deep fry meat on moderate to high heat until it becomes dry and crisp. Turn heat up during last stages of cooking to thoroughly crisp the meat slices. Remove from oil and drain on absorbent paper.

Shred green chillies and make flowers from red chillies by shredding the ends with a sharp knife and placing in a dish of iced water to make the 'petals' curl. Slice shallots very thinly and fry in a little oil until crisp.

Arrange dried beef slices on a serving plate. Scatter on sliced green chilli and fried shallots and decorate with chilli flowers.

PORK

MALACCAN DEVIL'S CURRY

This recipe came from an old resident of the Portuguese Village on the outskirts of the city of Malacca, where descendants of Portuguese settlers have congregated. Here they still carry on many of the old Portuguese traditions and retain some of the culture their ancestors brought to Malacca in the 16th century. This fiery 'Devil's' curry is an adaptation of the European 'Diable' or devilled dish.

750 g (1½ lb) pork shoulder, boneless
2 tablespoons white vinegar
1 tablespoon dark soya sauce
6 shallots or 3 small red onions
1 tablespoon oil
3 cloves garlic, crushed
4 cm (1½ inch) piece fresh ginger, sliced
2 teaspoons grated *lengkuas* (optional)
1 teaspoon dried shrimp paste
8-10 dried chillies, crushed
1 heaped teaspoon mustard seeds, lightly crushed
1 heaped teaspoon fenugreek seeds, lightly crushed
¾ teaspoon turmeric powder, or
    2 teaspoons grated fresh turmeric
1 stalk lemon grass, very finely chopped
6 candlenuts
1¼ cups veal or light beef stock
salt
pepper

Cut pork into 5 cm (2 inch) pieces and sprinkle with a mixture of vinegar and soya sauce. Leave to stand for 30 minutes.
　　Peel and chop shallots or onions. Heat oil in a large saucepan and fry shallots with crushed garlic for 2 minutes. Add sliced ginger, *lengkuas* (if used), dried shrimp paste, chillies and mustard and fenugreek seeds. Stir on moderate heat for 3 minutes, then add turmeric, lemon grass and ground candlenuts. Put in cubed meat and mix well with the seasonings. Turn heat up to brown meat well.
　　Pour in stock, season with salt and pepper and cover pan tightly. Cook on a moderate heat until meat is tender. Shake pan occasionally to turn meat, but do not open lid for at least the first 20 minutes of cooking.
　　If liquid dries up too quickly, sprinkle on a little more stock or water to keep meat moist until cooked. When meat is done, the liquid should be completely absorbed and the pan dry.

SPICED ROAST PORK

CHA SIEW

750 g (1½ lb) fat belly pork with rind
1 tablespoon coriander, ground
½ teaspoon black peppercorns, lightly crushed
¼ teaspoon cinnamon, ground
1 heaped teaspoon cummin, ground
1/8 teaspoon Chinese five-spice powder
2 cloves
2½ teaspoons light soya sauce
12 spring onions, finely chopped
2 teaspoons sugar
2 teaspoons salt
vinegar
lard or vegetable oil

Wipe pork and cut deep incisions into the skin diagonally. Grind together coriander, peppercorns, cinnamon, cummin, five-spice and cloves and mix with soya sauce, chopped spring onions, sugar and salt. Rub the seasonings well into the pork meat.

Put meat on a lightly greased baking tray and splash on a little vinegar. Set in a fairly hot oven (220°C/425°F/Gas Mark 7) and cook for 20 minutes, then pour in a little oil or melted lard and cover pan with a tightly fitted lid or a sheet of aluminium foil. Turn down oven to moderate (180°C/350°F/Gas Mark 4) and cook for approximately 2 hours until pork is very tender. Baste with a little oil and the pan juices every 15 minutes. If meat appears to be drying up, splash in a little water to keep moist.

When meat is done, remove from the oven and lift out from the tray. Allow to cool slightly, then cut into thin slices and serve immediately, or allow to cool completely and serve cold.

STEWED PORK RIBS

PAI GWAT

375 g (¾ lb) meaty pork ribs
2 tablespoons dark soya sauce
1 tablespoon light soya sauce
½ cup light stock
2-3 fresh red chillies, sliced
5 cm (2 inch) piece fresh ginger, shredded
1 tablespoon sugar
2 tablespoons oil

Trim ribs and chop into 4 cm (1½ inch) pieces. Place in a large bowl. Mix together all remaining ingredients, except oil. Pour over ribs and marinate for 1-1½ hours.

Drain pork, reserving marinade. Heat oil in a *wok* and stir-fry ribs for 3 minutes, then pour in marinade and cover pan. Simmer on low heat for 20 minutes, adding a little more water or stock if necessary. Serve as a main course or as part of a 'Dim Sum' meal.

Instead of frying, the ribs and marinade may be placed in a shallow dish inside a steamer and steamed over high heat for 25-30 minutes.

SATAY

ASSORTED SATAY

A renowned dish in Malaysia, Singapore and Indonesia, this delicious spiced meat or seafood on bamboo skewers is sold at roadside stalls, cafes and restaurants.

Makes 3 dozen.

1 tablespoon coriander, ground
1 teaspoon fennel, ground (optional)
1½ teaspoons cummin, ground
3 cloves garlic, crushed
2-3 dried chillies, soaked
1 stalk lemon grass, chopped
2.5 cm (1 inch) piece fresh ginger, chopped
2 teaspoons sugar
1 teaspoon tamarind
1 teaspoon turmeric powder
1 kg (2 lb) beef, mutton, pork, chicken and raw
    prawns (mixed)
salt
¼ cup thick coconut milk
1½ tablespoons oil
36 bamboo skewers
2 large cucumbers

Satay Sauce:
2 teaspoons coriander, ground
1 teaspoon cummin, ground
1 teaspoon fennel, ground
6 dried chillies, soaked
2 cloves garlic, chopped
3 shallots or 6 spring onions, chopped
1 heaped teaspoon dried shrimp paste
8 candlenuts
1 stalk lemon grass
1 tablespoon oil
155 g (5 oz) roasted peanuts, coarsely ground
¾ cup thick coconut milk
½ cup tamarind water, made with 2 teaspoons
    tamarind
sugar
salt

To prepare the Satay marinade, mix together coriander, fennel and cummin and roast briefly in a dry pan or under griller. Grind to a paste with garlic, chillies, lemon grass, ginger, sugar, tamarind and turmeric. Cut all meat into small thin pieces. Peel and devein prawns. Sprinkle with salt. Rub meat and prawns with the seasonings and stand for at least 1 hour to absorb flavours.

Prepare sauce. Grind coriander, cummin, fennel, chillies, garlic, shallots or spring onions, dried shrimp paste, candlenuts and lemon grass to a paste. Heat 1 tablespoon oil in pan and fry ground seasonings for 3 minutes. Add ground peanuts and stir in coconut milk slowly. Cook on moderate heat, stirring constantly, for 5 minutes.

Pour in tamarind water and add sugar and salt to taste. Bring almost to the boil, then turn heat down and simmer until oil begins to rise to the surface. Add a little more coconut milk or water if sauce becomes too thick.

Thread various types of meat and prawns onto separate bamboo skewers. Pour thick coconut milk and oil over the Satay and then place under a griller or over a charcoal fire to roast until done. The surface should be crisp and inside tender and juicy. Brush with a little more of the coconut milk and oil during cooking to prevent meat drying out.

Peel cucumbers or scrape with the prongs of a fork and rub with salt. Cut into 2.5 cm (1 inch) cubes and arrange on several plates. Serve cooked Satay with flat plates of sauce and the cucumber.

FISH ROLLS WITH SATAY SAUCE

This dish of fish rolls prepared Chinese style but served with a typical Malay sauce exemplifies the integration of cuisines in Malaysia and Singapore.

500 g (1 lb) fillets of cod, haddock or snapper
2 medium onions, minced
3 cloves garlic, minced
1 egg
1 tablespoon plain flour
2 teaspoons chopped fresh coriander leaves or parsley
salt
pepper
75 g (2½ oz) browned breadcrumbs
vegetable oil
Satay sauce

Mince or chop fish finely and blend to a smooth paste with onions and garlic. Blend in egg, flour, chopped coriander and season with salt and pepper. Knead till smooth, then form into rolls about 8 cm (3 inches) long and 2.5 cm (1 inch) thick.

Coat generously with breadcrumbs and deep fry in hot oil until a deep golden brown. Lift from oil and drain on absorbent paper.

Prepare Satay sauce as directed and serve in a separate dish. Serve fish rolls hot or cold.

VEGETABLES

MALAY VEGETABLE SALAD
PASEMBOR

155 g (5 oz) beanshoots
½ small cucumber
90 g (3 oz) yam bean *(bangkuang)*, or hard green pear
   or apple
12 lettuce leaves
1-2 hardboiled eggs
1 fresh red chilli
1 tablespoon peanut oil
1 cake hard beancurd
4 shallots or 1 medium red onion
sprigs of fresh coriander or mint

Sauce:
2 heaped tablespoons roasted peanuts
4 dried chillies, soaked
1 tablespoon sugar
pinch salt
1 teasooon dried shrimp paste
1 tablespoon tamarind
½ cup boiling water

Prepare sauce first. Grind peanuts coarsely. Pound chillies and add to the peanuts together with sugar and salt. Toast dried shrimp paste under a griller for 2 minutes, then mix with other ingredients. Soak tamarind in boiling water, then strain. Pour all sauce ingredients except tamarind water into a small saucepan and bring slowly to the boil. Stir in tamarind water and beat till sauce is smooth and rather thick. Pour into a sauce jug and serve separately.

   To prepare salad, clean beanshoots and scald with boiling water. Drain and allow to cool. Wipe cucumber and shred finely. Peel yam bean and shred very finely. Sprinkle with a little salt to prevent discolouration. Shred lettuce, slice boiled eggs and cut red chilli into very thin strips.

   Heat oil in a small frying pan and fry beancurd until golden. Cool and shred. Peel shallots or onion and slice thinly. Fry in a very little oil until slightly crisp. Remove and set aside as garnish. If green pear or apple is used, peel and slice thinly.

   Arrange shredded lettuce in a bed on a flat platter and top with beanshoots, cucumber, yam bean (or apple or pear), and shredded beancurd. Decorate with sliced egg and garnish with strips of chilli, fried shallots or onion and coriander or mint sprigs. Serve chilled.

FRUIT AND VEGETABLE SALAD

RUJAK

¼ yam bean *(bangkuang)*, or 1 hard green pear
2 tablespoons oil
1 cake hard beancurd
125 g (¼ lb) beanshoots
1 green mango, or 2 slices green papaya
1 star fruit (carambola), optional
1 small cucumber
6 lettuce leaves
6 thin slices pineapple

Sauce:
1 tablespoon tamarind
½ cup boiling water
2 fresh red chillies, minced
1 tablespoon roasted peanuts, crushed
½ teaspoon dried shrimp paste
1-2 teaspoons sugar
2 tablespoons sweet soya sauce

Prepare sauce first by infusing tamarind in boiling water until softened. Mash pulp, then strain into a small saucepan. Add chilli and peanuts, crumbled dried shrimp paste, sugar and sweet soya sauce. Bring almost to the boil. Check flavour and add more sugar if needed Pour into a sauce boat and set aside.
　Shred peeled yam bean (if used), and drop into boiling water. Leave for 10 minutes, then drain. If using pear, peel and shred and sprinkle with a little salt water.
　Heat oil and fry beancurd for 2 minutes, lift out and cool. Cut into thin slices. Steep beanshoots in boiling water for 2 minutes, then drain well. Rinse in cold water and drain again. Shred mango or papaya and thinly slice cucumber and star fruit (if used).
　Wash lettuce and arrange on a plate. Cut pineapple into small wedges and place around the edge of the dish. Stack all vegetables and fruit in the dish with beancurd on top. Pour on the sauce or serve separately.

CUCUMBER SALAD

2 medium cucumbers
1 small red onion, finely chopped
2 candlenuts
1 teaspoon fresh grated turmeric or
　⅓ teaspoon turmeric powder
2.5 cm (1 inch) piece fresh ginger, shredded
½ tablespoon oil
2 teaspoons sugar
salt
6 spring onions, shredded
1 tablespoon coarsely ground roasted peanuts
fresh red and green chilli, shredded

Wipe cucumbers and cut lengthways into quarters then into 2.5 cm (1 inch) pieces. Sprinkle lightly with salt.
　Pound onion to a paste with candlenuts, turmeric and ginger. Heat oil in a saucepan and fry ground seasonings for 3 minutes before adding cucumber, sugar and salt. Fry on moderate heat until cucumber softens slightly.
　Mix in shredded spring onions and spoon into a deep serving dish. Garnish with ground peanuts and decorate with shredded red and green chilli. Serve cold.

FRIED BEANCURD SQUARES
TAUKWA GORENG

3 green chillies
1 fresh red chilli
1 clove garlic
2 tablespoons brown sugar
1 tablespoon dark soya sauce
1 tablespoon white wine vinegar
1 teaspoon cummin, ground
½ cup water
155 g (5 oz) roasted peanuts, crushed
salt
6 squares hard beancurd
60 g (2 oz) beanshoots
1 small cucumber
peanut oil

Chop chillies and garlic finely and mix with brown sugar, soya sauce, vinegar, cummin and cold water. Stir in crushed peanuts and add salt. Cook on moderate heat for 10 minutes, stirring frequently. Keep warm while beancurd is prepared.

Cut beancurd squares into 3 slices, horizontally. Heat 1 cm (½ inch) oil and carefully lower in several beancurd squares. Fry for 3-4 minutes. Lift out and place on a serving plate and keep warm.

Wash and dry cucumber, rub with salt and shred or grate. Remove roots and tops from beanshoots and scald with boiling water. Arrange a little shredded cucumber and several beanshoots on top of each beancurd slice.

Reheat sauce and spoon a little onto each beancurd square before serving.

VEGETABLES IN COCONUT MILK

185 g (6 oz) green beans
250 g (½ lb) Chinese cabbage or white cabbage
1½ large onions
2 medium tomatoes
2 fresh red chillies
2 tablespoons vegetable oil
2 cloves garlic, crushed
⅓ teaspoon turmeric powder
½ teaspoon chilli powder (optional)
salt
1¼ cups thin coconut milk
1 tablespoon tamarind water, made with 1½ teaspoons tamarind

Cut beans into 5 cm (2 inch) lengths. Chop Chinese cabbage and wash, shake out excess water. Chop onions roughly, peel and chop tomatoes and slice chillies.

Heat oil in a frying pan and add garlic and chopped onion. Fry for 2 minutes, then put in beans, turmeric, chilli powder (if used), sliced chillies and salt. Pour in ½ cup coconut milk and stir well. Cook on moderate heat for 5 minutes, then add cabbage and cook for a further 4 minutes.

Pour on remaining coconut milk, bring almost to the boil and turn heat down low. Add tomato and tamarind water and simmer for 1-2 minutes. Stir continually to prevent coconut sauce curdling. Add salt to taste.

Nonya laksa with coconut sauce (recipe page 43).

FRIED EGGPLANT
PAGRI TERONG

3-4 medium eggplants, about 375 g (¾ lb) total weight
salt
oil
6 spring onions, sliced
8 cloves garlic, crushed
2 teaspoons grated *lengkuas*
2 fresh green chillies, thinly sliced
1½ teaspoons cummin, ground
3 black cardamoms, crushed
2.5 cm (1 inch) stick cinnamon
1 teaspoon fennel, crushed
2 tablespoons mild curry paste
1 fresh red chilli, sliced
1 cup thick coconut milk

Wipe eggplants and slice into quarters lengthways, from base to stem, leaving stem section intact. Sprinkle with salt and stand for 4-5 minutes to draw bitter juices. Rinse and wipe dry.

Heat 5 cm (2 inches) oil to smoking point and fry eggplants until soft, turning heat down after first minute. Drain and cool. Pour off all but 1 tablespoon oil and fry onions and garlic for 2 minutes. Add ginger and chillies and fry for a further minute, then add all spices, curry paste and chilli and fry for 4 minutes. Pour on coconut milk, add salt to taste and stir well.

Return eggplants to the pan and cook for 10 minutes on low heat. Serve warm or cold as a main course or side dish.

MIXED VEGETABLES WITH SALTED BLACK BEANS

500 g (1 lb) mixed green vegetables
3 cloves garlic
2 tablespoons oil
8 shallots or 3 small red onions, thinly sliced
3 fresh red chillies, sliced
2½ teaspoons salted black beans, crushed
1½ teaspoons sugar
⅓ cup water
3 teaspoons light soya sauce
salt

Use such vegetables as long beans, green beans, green peas, cabbage, Chinese cabbage, spinach. Chop all vegetables, wash and drain well. Parboil peas (if used).

Crush garlic and fry gently in oil, then add shallots or onion. Stir-fry for 2 minutes before adding chillies, crushed black beans and sugar. Pour on water, soya sauce and add the vegetables. Stir-fry for 1 minute, then cover pan and simmer for 4-5 minutes, depending on type of vegetables used.

When ready the vegetables should be lightly cooked but retaining crispness. Add salt to taste. For extra flavour include chopped shrimp or chicken meat.

37

Fried rice noodles (Behoon) (recipe page 44).

STUFFED BEANCURD, PEPPERS AND BLACK MUSHROOMS

6 pieces hard beancurd, each 5 cm (2 inches) square
6 green peppers, no more than 5 cm (2 inches) in
  diameter
6 medium sized dried black mushrooms, soaked
250 g (½ lb) lean pork
125 g (¼ lb) small peeled raw shrimp
1 cm (½ inch) piece fresh ginger, shredded
3 spring onions, shredded
1 tablespoon oil or lard
2 egg whites
1½ tablespoons dark soya sauce
2 teaspoons Chinese wine
½ teaspoon white pepper
pinch monosodium glutamate (optional)
vegetable or peanut oil
⅔ cup beef stock
1 teaspoon cornflour
1½ teaspoons sesame oil

Cut beancurd in halves or into triangular pieces and
make a slit in each. Wipe peppers and cut in halves
horizontally. Remove seeds. Remove stems from mushrooms.

Chop pork and shrimps very finely, or mince, and
mix into a paste with ginger and spring onion. Blend in
melted lard or oil. Bind with egg white and season with
soya sauce, Chinese wine, pepper and monosodium
glutamate (if used). Knead to a smooth paste.

Place about 1 tablespoonful of stuffing into each
pepper half, 2 teaspoonsful into each mushroom top
and 1 teaspoonful into the slit of each piece of beancurd. Place stuffed mushrooms in a steamer on a piece
of waxed paper and steam for 12-15 minutes.

While mushrooms are cooking, heat oil and fry stuffed beancurd and peppers for 5-6 minutes. Remove
from oil, drain and keep warm.

Drain oil from pan and pour in stock. Bring to the
boil, adjust seasoning if necessary, then thicken with
cornflour mixed with a little cold water. Cook until
sauce thickens and clears.

Arrange steamed mushrooms, fried beancurd and
peppers decoratively on a serving plate. Pour on hot
stock and sprinkle with sesame oil.

LADIES FINGERS

375 g (¾ lb) ladies fingers (okra), about 8-10 cm
  (3-4 inches) long
salt
pepper
1 teaspoon chilli powder
1 teaspoon cummin, ground

Wash ladies fingers, wipe dry and remove stems with a
sharp knife. Carve tops into a point around the bases of
the stems. Make several lengthways incisions in each
ladies finger without cutting tops or bottoms. Sprinkle
with salt and stand for 5 minutes. Rinse in warm water
and wipe dry.

Place ladies fingers in a saucepan with salt, pepper,
chilli and cummin. Cover with water and simmer on
moderate heat till tender. Drain and serve hot or cold as
a side dish.

RICE

COCONUT RICE
NASI LEMAK

375 g (¾ lb) long grain rice
½ cup thick coconut milk
2¼ cups thin coconut milk
2 teaspoons salt
2 eggs
sliced onion or onion sambal
sliced cucumber
dried salted whitebait *(ikan bilis)*

Wash rice and pour into a saucepan with thick coconut milk. Cook on moderate heat for 10 minutes, stirring frequently. Pour on thin coconut milk and salt, cover and bring to the boil. Reduce heat and cook until rice is tender and coconut milk absorbed.

Beat eggs and pour into a very lightly oiled pan. Swirl pan to make omelette as thin as possible. Cook until firm, then remove and leave to cool. Shred finely.

Wash salt fish and dry thoroughly. Fry in hot oil until very crisp. Drain well. Spoon cooked rice into a serving bowl and garnish with fried salt fish and shredded omelette. Arrange sliced onion and cucumber around the rice, and serve onion sambal in a separate dish.

YELLOW RICE

½ teaspoon saffron strands
2 tablespoons boiling water
345 g (11 oz) long grain rice
3 tablespoons *ghee*
2 teaspoons salt
tomato wedges
fresh coriander sprigs

Steep saffron in boiling water. Wash rice well, drain and allow to dry for at least 20 minutes, preferably longer.

Heat *ghee* in a large, heavy-bottomed saucepan and put in the rice. Fry on moderate heat for 5 minutes, stirring to coat each rice grain. Cover with 2.5 cm (1 inch) water above the level of the rice, strain saffron and add tinted water to the rice. Add salt and stir well. Bring to the boil, cover and turn heat down very low. Simmer until rice is tender and all liquid absorbed. Leave to stand for a further 10 minutes, covered, but off the heat.

Spoon into a serving dish and garnish with tomato wedges and coriander sprigs.

FRIED RICE
NASI GORENG

6 spring onions, sliced
4 fresh red chillies, sliced
vegetable oil
2 slices ham or bacon
185 g (6 oz) peeled prawns
750 g (1½ lb) cold cooked white rice
2 teaspoons dark soya sauce
salt
2 eggs, lightly beaten
2 tablespoons finely chopped celery leaves (optional)
3-4 spring onions, chopped
100 g (3½ oz) cooked peas
1½ teaspoons chilli powder

Lightly fry spring onions and chillies in 2 tablespoons oil. Chop bacon or ham and prawns and add to the pan. Stir-fry for 2 minutes. Pour in rice, mixing well with meat. Add more oil if necessary. Sprinkle on soya sauce and salt to taste. Stir-fry rice on moderate heat until rice changes colour and is slightly crisp. Remove and keep warm.

Wipe out pan and pour in beaten egg, swirling pan to make a very thin omelette. Cook until set, then remove and shred. Add celery (if used), and a little more oil and stir-fry for 2 minutes. Add chopped spring onions and green peas and heat through, then return rice to the pan and stir in chilli powder. Add salt and more soya sauce if necessary. Stir on high heat for 1 minute, then spoon into a serving dish and garnish with shredded egg.

NOODLES

HOKKIEN FRIED NOODLES

8 cups chicken stock
1 kg (2 lb) fresh thick egg noodles or
   375 g (¾ lb) spaghetti
2½ tablespoons peanut oil
1 medium onion, finely chopped
4 cloves garlic, minced
2 tablespoons dried shrimp, soaked overnight
185 g (6 oz) small peeled raw shrimps
250 g (½ lb) beanshoots
2 teaspoons chilli powder
salt
pepper
1 fresh red chilli, shredded
125 g (¼ lb) cooked shrimps or prawns, chopped
2 hardboiled eggs

Sauce:
2 medium onions
2 tablespoons oil
100 g (3½ oz) raw prawns, finely chopped
2 squares soft beancurd, diced
1½ cups chicken or fish stock
1-2 fresh red chillies, chopped
dark soya sauce to taste
salt
pepper
1 teaspoon cornflour

Bring chicken stock to the boil and drop in noodles. Cook for about 8 minutes until tender but not soft. Drain, and spread on a tray to cool and dry.

Prepare sauce. Fry chopped onions in oil for 2 minutes, then add chopped prawns and diced beancurd and cook on moderate heat for 3-4 minutes. Pour in chicken or fish stock and add chopped chilli. Bring to the boil, lower heat and cook for 10 minutes. Season with soya sauce, salt and pepper. Thicken with cornflour mixed with a little cold water, stirring till sauce thickens and clears. Set aside, keeping warm.

Heat oil in a frying pan or *wok* and fry chopped onion and garlic until golden, then add drained dried shrimps and fresh shrimps, both finely chopped. Saute for 3 minutes before adding noodles and beanshoots. Saute for a further 3 minutes, then stir in chilli powder and salt and pepper to taste.

Arrange noodles on a large serving plate, garnish with shredded chilli and cooked shrimp or prawns and arrange sliced boiled eggs around the edge of the plate. Reheat sauce and serve separately, or pour over noodles just before serving.

Note: If Hokkien Fried Noodles is to be served with other main dishes, reduce quantity by at least half.

FRIED RICE NOODLES
CHA KWAY TEOW

850 g (1¾ lb) fresh rice flour noodles *(kway teow)*
100 g (3½ oz) raw prawns
60 g (2 oz) hard sausages or Chinese sausages
100 g (3½ oz) spinach or mustard greens
250 g (½ lb) beanshoots
vegetable oil or melted lard
60 g (2 oz) shredded cuttlefish or squid
125 g (¼ lb) chicken breast or pork meat, diced
3 cloves garlic
2 heaped teaspoons sugar
2 tablespoons oyster sauce
4 spring onions
2 tablespoons dark soya sauce
2 tablespoons light soya sauce
white pepper
monosodium glutamate (optional)
2 eggs (optional)
fresh chilli, chopped
spring onions, chopped
chilli sauce

Soak *kway teow* noodles in cold water for 3 minutes. Drain and spread on a tray covered with a cloth to dry.

Peel and devein prawns, and cut into small pieces. Dice sausage. Rinse mustard greens or spinach, shake out water and cut into 5 cm (2 inch) pieces. Steep beanshoots in boiling water for 2-3 minutes, then drain well and set aside.

Heat 1 tablespoon oil or lard and fry prawns, cuttlefish, chicken or pork and sausage for 3 minutes. Remove and set aside, keeping warm. Add another tablespoon oil and fry mustard greens or spinach and beanshoots for 1 minute. Remove and mix with the cooked meat.

Add more oil or lard and fry crushed garlic. Cut *kway teow* noodles into 15 cm (6 inch) pieces for easier handling and drop into the pan. Stir-fry for 4-5 minutes until slightly crisped on the edges. Sprinkle on sugar, oyster sauce, shredded spring onions and soya sauce.

Season with white pepper and monosodium glutamate (if used), then add cooked meat and vegetables. Stir all together and cook for a further 2 minutes. If using eggs, break onto noodles and stir in. Turn heat off immediately. Lift onto a large serving plate and garnish with chopped chilli and spring onion. Serve with small dishes of chilli sauce.

Note: If *kway teow* is to be served with several other dishes reduce the quantity by about half.

NONYA LAKSA WITH COCONUT SAUCE

LAKSA LEMAK

6 candlenuts
4 fresh red chillies
1 large onion, minced
5 cm (2 inch) piece fresh ginger, minced
2 cloves garlic, minced
1 tablespoon oil
1½ teaspoons turmeric powder
1 teaspoon coriander, ground
1½ teaspoons dried shrimp paste
1 stalk lemon grass, chopped
1 medium tomato, chopped
2 teaspoons sugar
1½ teaspoons salt
½ teaspoon white pepper
185 g (6 oz) white fish fillets
90 g (3 oz) peeled raw shrimp
⅔ cup water
¾ cup thick coconut milk
9 cups thin coconut milk
500 g (1 lb) thin rice vermicelli
185 g (6 oz) beanshoots
90 g (3 oz) fried hard beancurd, shredded
8 cm (3 inch) piece young cucumber, shredded
4 lettuce leaves, shredded
8 spring onions, chopped
sprigs fresh mint
1 fresh red chilli, shredded finely
1 ginger flower, shredded (optional)

Grind candlenuts and red chillies to a paste. Mix with minced onion, ginger and garlic.

Heat oil and fry seasonings for 2 minutes, then add turmeric, coriander, dried shrimp paste, lemon grass, chopped tomato and sugar. Season with salt and pepper. Cook for 3 minutes then set aside.

Cut fish fillets into 2 cm (¾ inch) dice and place in a small saucepan with shrimp. Cover with water and boil for 10 minutes. Strain, reserving liquid and meat. Set aside to cool.

Pour thick coconut milk into a large saucepan and add fried seasonings. Stir well and when liquid begins to boil, pour in thin coconut milk and fish stock. Bring almost to the boil again, add fish and shrimp and turn heat down. Simmer for 5 minutes. Add salt and pepper to taste.

Place vermicelli in a large bowl and cover with boiling water. Allow to stand for 8-10 minutes to soften. Steep beanshoots in boiling water for 2 minutes, drain and rinse in cold water. Drain noodles and beanshoots.

Into each bowl place a serving of noodles, then top with beanshoots, shredded beancurd, cucumber, lettuce and a little shredded ginger flower (if used). Pour on enough coconut sauce to cover and garnish with chopped spring onion, mint leaves and shredded chilli.

FRIED RICE NOODLES

BEEHOON

375 g (¾ lb) thin rice vermicelli
2 cloves garlic
1½ teaspoons coriander, ground
½ teaspoon turmeric powder
peanut oil
8 dried Chinese mushrooms, soaked
90 g (3 oz) peeled raw prawns
125 g (¼ lb) white fish
2 medium onions
4 fresh red chillies
salt
125 g (¼ lb) beanshoots
2 eggs, lightly beaten
3 spring onions, chopped
fresh coriander sprigs

Soak noodles in cold water for 5 minutes, then drop into boiling water and steep for about 6-10 minutes until soft. Drain well and rinse in cold water.

Crush garlic and make into a paste with coriander and turmeric. Heat 1 tablespoon oil in a *wok* or frying pan and fry seasoning paste for 2 minutes.

Remove mushroom stems and slice mushrooms thinly. Chop prawns and fish into small dice and add to the pan together with mushrooms. Fry on moderate heat for 4 minutes. Remove from pan and keep warm.

Add 2 tablespoons oil to the pan and fry sliced onions and chillies. Add noodles, season with salt and stir thoroughly. Scatter beanshoots on top and cook, covered, for 1 minute. Mix beanshoots into noodles and remove from pan. Pour in beaten egg, swirling pan to make a very thin omelette. Cook until set, then remove and cool slightly. Shred.

Reheat noodles, adding half the seafood and mushrooms and half of the shredded egg to the pan. Lift onto a flat serving dish and garnish with remaining seafood and mushrooms. Top with shredded egg, chopped spring onions and coriander sprigs.

NOODLES WITH SOUR FISH SAUCE

LAKSA ASAM

2 cups boiling water
3 tablespoons tamarind
375 g (¾ lb) fish fillets
7 cups cold water
4 fresh red chillies
12 spring onions
1 tablespoon sugar
1½ teaspoons dried shrimp paste
2.5 cm (1 inch) piece lemon grass, finely chopped
2 teaspoons fresh grated turmeric, or
    ¾ teaspoon turmeric powder
salt
pepper
250 g (½ lb) thin rice vermicelli
250 g (½ lb) fresh egg noodles, or
    thick rice flour noodles
8 shallots or 2 medium red onions, thinly sliced
1 ginger flower (optional)
1 small bunch fresh mint leaves
1 small bunch fresh basil leaves (optional)

Pour boiling water over tamarind and allow to stand for at least 15 minutes. Put fish fillets in a saucepan, cover with cold water and bring to the boil. Simmer until fish is soft and flaky. Strain, reserving stock and fish.

Finely slice or mince chillies and spring onions. Add to the fish stock with sugar, dried shrimp paste, lemon grass and turmeric. Bring to the boil, season with salt and pepper and simmer for 10 minutes.

Soak rice vermicelli in boiling water to soften. Soak egg noodles or thick rice noodles in cold water for 10 minutes. Drain, put into a saucepan, cover with slightly salted water and bring to the boil. Reduce heat and cook until tender. Drain and rinse both lots of noodles. Divide noodles between six large bowls and top with flaked fish and sliced shallots or red onion.

Pour fish sauce over noodles and garnish with finely shredded ginger flower (if used), sprigs of mint and sweet basil. Strain tamarind through a piece of muslin and serve tamarind juice in a jug, or pour over noodles before serving.

ACCOMPANIMENTS

SAMBALS

Sambals are accompaniments served in small dishes, usually several at a time, with every Malaysian meal. They add flavour and extra heat to meals. The following three sambals are typical examples.

Other sambals could also be prepared to serve with curries and spiced dishes: grated fresh or desiccated coconut, sliced banana, sliced onion, lemon or lime wedges, raisins, dry fried onions, sliced cucumber, roasted peanuts, sliced omelette, fried dry fish, Bombay duck, or wedges of pineapple. Prepare several and serve in small flat dishes or sauce bowls.

ONION SAMBAL

4 medium onions
2 cloves garlic
½ cup white vinegar
2 teaspoons sugar

Peel onions and slice thinly. Pull into rings. Crush garlic and sprinkle over onions. Pour on vinegar and dust with sugar. Marinate for at least 15 minutes before serving. Drain off vinegar before serving, if preferred.

CHILLI SAMBAL

3 green chillies
2 teaspoons salt
1-2 teaspoons sugar
¼ cup white vinegar

Wipe chillies, remove stems and slice thinly. Remove seeds for milder *sambal*. Sprinkle salt and sugar onto vinegar, stirring until dissolved. Pour over chilli and stand for at least 3 hours before using.

TOMATO SAMBAL

4 large tomatoes, diced
1 large onion, minced
2 green chillies, minced
1 tablespoon white vinegar
1½ tablespoons sugar
½ teaspoon salt

Mix all ingredients, adding more salt or sugar to taste. Let stand for 15 minutes before serving.
flesh finely. Mix with coriander or celery leaves, spring onions, salt and pepper. Knead to a smooth paste with oil and a little cold water. With oiled hands form fish paste into small balls by squeezing the paste from a clenched hand out between curled thumb and forefinger. Drop into a bowl of cold, salted water.

Heat oil in a large pot and fry ginger for 1 minute. Pour in fish stock, salt and pepper, chilli powder and add washed vegetables. Drop in drained fish balls and simmer for 12-15 minutes. Garnish with shredded chilli.

MANGO CHUTNEY

6 medium size green mangoes
6 dried chillies
2.5 cm (1 inch) fresh ginger, shredded
1 teaspoon chilli powder
1 teaspoon black peppercorns, crushed lightly
½ cup vinegar
1 cup sugar
3 teaspoons salt
2 cloves garlic, crushed
½ cup water
1 tablespoon raisins, soaked in water

Peel and slice mangoes, discarding stones. Grind or crumble chillies and mix with shredded ginger, chilli and peppercorns.

Boil vinegar, sugar and salt, and add chilli paste, crushed garlic and water. Cook for 2 minutes, then add sliced mango. Simmer for 10-12 minutes, and add drained raisins. Remove from heat and transfer to a wide-necked jar. Seal tightly.

This chutney can be used immediately, but will develop more flavour after several days. Can be stored for many weeks.

COCONUT CHUTNEY

8 dried chillies
3 teaspoons dried fish floss, or powdered dried shrimps
3 shallots or 1 small red onion, chopped
salt
100 g (3½ oz) grated fresh coconut, or
    75 g (2½ oz) desiccated coconut
lemon or lime juice

Grind dried chillies, dried fish or shrimp, shallots and salt to a paste. Add coconut, ground slightly, or desiccated coconut moistened with a little warm water. Moisten with lemon or lime juice and a little water if necessary.

Stir well to thoroughly mix all ingredients. Allow to stand for several hours before using.

DESSERTS

SWEET POTATO DESSERT
BUBOR CHA CHA

1 quantity green pea flour 'beans' (see Cendol)
1 medium sweet potato or yam
1 teaspoon salt
3 cups thick coconut milk
8 cm (3 inch) block palm sugar *(gula Melaka)*, or
    185 g (6 oz) brown sugar
1 *pandan* leaf (optional)
⅔ cup water
shaved or crushed ice

Prepare green pea flour beans and cool.
Steam sweet potato or yam until tender, but not too
soft. Cut into 0.5 cm (¼ inch) dice. Chill. Stir salt into
coconut milk.
Crumble palm sugar into a saucepan, add water and
pandan leaf and simmer until sugar is completely dissolved. Strain and discard leaf. If brown sugar is used
pour into a small saucepan with water and bring to the
boil. Cook until colour has changed to a deep golden
brown and the syrup is very sticky. Remove from heat,
cover hand and carefully pour in ⅓ cup cold water.
Chill.
Into small glass bowls place a spoonful each of diced
sweet potato or yam, green pea flour 'beans' and
crushed ice. Pour in a generous amount of sugar syrup
and coconut milk.

GULA MELAKA PUDDING

125 g (¼ lb) pearl sago
4½ cups water
155 g (5 oz) crumbled palm sugar *(gula Melaka)*, or
    185 g (6 oz) brown sugar
¾ cup hot water
1 *pandan* leaf (optional)
1¼ cups thick coconut milk

Wash sago, drain, and put into a saucepan. Add water
and bring to the boil. Turn heat down and cook until
sago is tender and each grain clear. Rinse with several
lots of cold water to separate grains, then divide between small glass bowls or jelly moulds and place in the
refrigerator to chill.
Put palm sugar into a small pan, add crushed *pandan*
leaf (if used), and pour on hot water. Simmer for 6
minutes. Strain and discard leaf.
If brown sugar is used, place in a small saucepan with
⅔ cup water and bring to the boil. Stir to dissolve sugar
and cook on high heat until syrup is quite sticky and has
begun to caramelise to a deep brown. Remove from
heat. Carefully pour in ¼ cup cold water, holding
saucepan well away to avoid burns from the spluttering
syrup. Cover hands with a cloth before doing this. Stir
well and allow to cool, then chill.
To serve dessert, pour a little sugar syrup and coconut
milk over each dish of sago. Add a little shaved ice if
desired. Garnish with a mint leaf.

A selection of sambals (recipes pages 46 and 47).

CENDOL

This is a very special sweet also popular in Indonesia. It can be served as a drink or dessert. The sweet coconut milk makes it a great palate soother after hot dishes.

60 g (2 oz) coloured or plain green pea flour, or
    arrowroot
1⅓ cups water
green or red food colouring (optional)
8 cm (3 inch) block palm sugar *(gula Melaka)*, or
    155 g (5 oz) brown sugar
⅔ cup hot water
1 crushed *pandan* leaf (optional)
7 cups thin coconut milk
shaved ice

Mix green pea flour or arrowroot with water and cook slowly, stirring to prevent lumps forming, until mixture is very thick and clear. If using plain green pea flour or arrowroot, colour half the mixture pink and the remainder green.

Push through a coarse strainer held over a basin of iced water. The mixture will break up into small bean-shaped lumps. Allow to cool, then drain. Alternatively spread thinly over a slightly chilled flat dish, or baking sheet and allow to set, then cut into very small pieces.

Crumble palm sugar into a small saucepan, add *pandan* leaf and pour on hot water. Simmer on low heat until sugar is dissolved, discard leaf, strain syrup and cool.

If brown sugar is used, pour into a small saucepan with ½ cup water. Bring to the boil and cook until it turns a deep golden colour and is very sticky. Remove from heat and carefully pour in 2¼ cups water, covering hand first to prevent burns. Stir in, cool and then chill.

Into large tall glasses pour about 1 tablespoon sugar syrup, 2 heaped tablespoons pea flour 'beans', a scoop of shaved ice and fill up with coconut milk. Serve with long straws and long-handled sundae spoons.

WAFFLE CAKES
KUEH BELANDA

10 eggs
345 g (11 oz) sugar
575 g (1 1/8 lb) plain flour, sifted
1 teaspoon Chinese five-spice powder
⅓ cup pure coconut oil, or vegetable oil
1¼-1½ cups water

Beat eggs lightly, add sugar and beat firmly. Blend in flour, five-spice powder and coconut or vegetable oil. Add enough water to form a batter of medium to thin consistency. Stand for at least 5 hours. Stir in very little more water before cooking. Beat for 3 minutes.

Heat a 15 cm (6 inch) waffle pan, oil lightly and pour in enough batter to make a 12-15 cm (5-6 inch) pancake. Cook over high heat until cakes are golden brown, turning once. Serve hot with butter or cold with honey or jam.

Cendol, gula melaka pudding, and sweet potato dessert
(recipes this page).

GLOSSARY

BAMBOO SHOOTS: Cream-coloured spear-like shoots of the bamboo plant. Fresh shoots must be peeled to the firm heart and then boiled. Also sold canned in water or in a sauce usually based on soya. Store in the refrigerator in a dish of fresh water, changing the water daily, for up to ten days. Winter bamboo shoots have a better flavour than the common variety.

BANGKUANG: Yam bean, a large tuberous root used as a vegetable.

BEANCURD: Soft beancurd is prepared by setting a liquid of ground soya beans with gypsum. Hard beancurd, or beancurd cake, is soft beancurd compressed to remove most of the water content.

BEEHOON: Very fine threads of rice vermicelli. When deep fried they puff up quite dramatically and become very crisp. Also served in soups and in well-sauced dishes.

CANDLENUTS: White waxy nuts similar to macadamia nuts. Used to add body and flavour to sauces.

COCONUT MILK: The thick and creamy liquid made from the ground flesh of ripe coconuts mixed with water. Not to be confused with coconut water, which is the almost clear liquid found inside the nut.

CURRY PASTE: Commercially prepared curry paste containing a mixture of spices in an oil or coconut-milk base.

CURRY POWDER: In Malaysia and Singapore, where curry is a main part of the diet, cooks prepare fresh spices daily and seldom use commercially prepared spice mixtures.

DAUN KESOM: A very pungent dark-green leaf.

FISH FLOSS: Shredded dried salt fish, or fish cooked to dryness in coconut milk and then finely shredded.

GHEE: Clarified butter, giving a richness to sweet and savoury dishes. It is high in cholesterol, and vegetable oils can be substituted.

KRUPUK: Small crisp wafers, generally made of prawns. Fry in hot oil for a few seconds until they puff up.

KWAY TEOW: Rice-flour noodles cut into flat strands.

LENGKUAS: A member of the ginger family with a similar though more delicate flavour and a creamy or pinkish flesh.

POPPY SEEDS, WHITE: Used as a flavouring and thickening ingredient.

SAFFRON: Imparts a delicate flavour and a bright orange-yellow colour.

SALTED BLACK BEANS: Preserved, fermented salted soya beans used as a well-flavoured seasoning ingredient in Malaysian cooking.

TAMARIND: Semi-dried flesh from the seed pods of the tamarind tree. Mix with hot water to make a strongly flavoured acidulating liquid for tenderising meats and for adding a sourish tang. Substitute vinegar, lime or lemon juice mixed with a little water.

INDEX